A Guide to Integrated Assurance

A Guide to Integrated Assurance

Association for Project Management

Association for Project Management
Ibis House, Regent Park
Summerleys Road, Princes Risborough
Buckinghamshire
HP27 9LE

British Library Cataloguing in Publication Data is available.
Paperback ISBN: 978-1-903494-04-2
EPUB ISBN: 978-1-903494-02-8

Cover design by Fountainhead Creative Consultants
Typeset by RefineCatch Limited, Bungay, Suffolk
in 11/14pt Foundry Sans

Contents

Figures and tables

Figures

Tables

Foreword

Integrated assurance is one of those things like risk, quality and benefits that only get noticed when things go wrong, when they are missing or when they are poorly executed.

Treating them separately in order to examine them has inadvertently allowed some people to treat them as optional extras. They are not. They answer the questions: Is it being done properly? What needs to be done to fix it?

Integrated assurance allows all stakeholders a view on what is happening and allows them the possibility of contributing to a successful outcome. Whether they want to contribute, or see the need to do so, is cultural and that is another story.

The Assurance Specific Interest Group (SIG), under Roy Millard's guidance, has produced a comprehensive encapsulation of the type of framework you need to have in place in order to make integrated assurance work for you.

Think hard before you say you don't need it. And if you have doubts or need help then talk it over with the Assurance SIG. Get involved and help APM to help you.

Steve Wake,
APM Chairman

Contributors

This guide was produced by a working group of the APM's Assurance SIG, the main authors of which are listed below:

Tony Atkins, previously BP Group Technology
Tere Bowers, Department for Work and Pensions
David Bright, BMT Group Ltd.
Alex Clark, Barclaycard
Helen Dagley, Midland Heart
Andrew Elliott, The Nichols Group
Phil Kemp, Major Projects Authority, Cabinet Office
Roy Millard, Transport for London
Paul Monaghan, Local Partnerships
Mark Reilly, EC Harris
Naveed Sheikh, Safran Power UK
David Small, LV=
Mark Sudan, Her Majesty's Revenue & Customs
Chris Watson, Nuclear Decommissioning Authority
David Youll, Sensus

The SIG is also grateful for input to the guide's development from:
Jane Rumsam, Programme & Project Assurance, Houses of Parliament
Amerjit Walia, Thames Valley University

Executive summary

Assurance exists to support the delivery of successful projects by providing analysis and peer challenge to the project team's approach. It should focus on increasing the likelihood of a successful project outcome. The process will normally evaluate project documentation and engage with key stakeholders, thereby allowing an independent assessment from their perspective of the project. It should contribute to their level of understanding and, through this, induce confidence in the project.

Having a long and diverse list of assurance providers may not necessarily be a problem. They may be quite necessary and may each be providing a different perspective. However, there is a risk of duplication between assurance providers that can lead to projects developing a feeling of assurance 'overload'. This can also result in projects being confused over the different types of assurance, and spending too much time supporting assurance and not delivering. In addition, the extent of assurance does not guarantee the avoidance of assurance gaps and can lead to confusion if mixed or contradictory opinions are given.

Projects may be impacted by external factors (i.e. the environment) and so it makes sense that the project's assurance plan needs to remain 'dynamic' and be continuously reviewed throughout the life of the project.

In summary, the benefits of an integrated assurance approach are:

- Assurance based on a comprehensive and shared view of risk enables a sponsor and other stakeholders to identify assurance needs effectively.
- Planning and coordinating assurance activities avoids assurance gaps and over-laps, and enables efficient use of resources for both assurers and the project.
- Integration enables the assurance to focus on key risks and controls.
- In providing an effective and appropriate governance hierarchy, it enables more direct attention to important exposures, areas not well covered and interrelationships across the whole project portfolio.
- Motivation, development and a sense of purpose among assurance providers are more readily facilitated.

1

Introduction

Assurance is an integral component of robust project governance as well as for governance of project management across an organisation. Through assurance, projects will undergo a range of reviews at different stages in their lifecycle. Integrated assurance is the co-ordination of these project reviews to ensure maximum impact and benefit at minimum cost and disruption. Only by having a systematic approach to assurance can an organisation hope to gain the full benefit of its assurance regime. Thus, a project assurance approach should be directly linked to an organisation's overall assurance strategy.

This guide aims to assist organisations in developing and implementing this integrated approach. It does not attempt to give guidance on assurance generally, as it assumes the reader is familiar with the topic.

For brevity, the guide uses the terms project and project management as inclusive of programmes and the management of programmes of projects.

1.1 The case for integrated assurance

This section begins by describing assurance, and then discusses the dimensions and benefits of integrated assurance in the project/programme context.

> *Assurance is the process of providing confidence to stakeholders that projects, programmes and portfolios will achieve their scope, time, cost and quality objectives, and realise their benefits*
> (APM Body of Knowledge 6th edition)

From this statement, it can be seen that the purpose of assurance is to give stakeholders confidence that their project objectives will be achieved. Assurance activities need to examine the ways in which risks and issues are being identified and managed. They also need to look at the way in which opportunities are being evaluated and the actions being taken to realise any benefits. Effective assurance gives stakeholders confidence that resources are not being wasted or potential value lost as a result of shortcomings in the execution of the project while achieving its agreed objectives. Assurance activities can also help identify

1

any shortcomings early enough for them to be rectified without an unfortunate impact on the project objectives.

There are a broad range of activities that may be carried out for various different stakeholders under this heading of assurance. Such activities all absorb time and money, and so could reduce the potential value of the project. In addition, the volume of assurance does not guarantee the avoidance of assurance gaps and can lead to confusion if mixed or contradictory opinions are given. Sometimes there is strength in welcoming different perspectives because of the different natures of assurance and the degree of objectivity exercised. The dialogue around reconciling those different views is what good governance is all about. If we seek one view on everything, we will compromise or dilute the assurance, thereby harming objectivity and devaluing the process.

The concept of integrated assurance is to streamline these disparate activities for greater efficiency and overall benefit for the project and its stakeholders. Integration of assurance can be considered across four dimensions.

1. *Multiple stakeholders*. Stakeholders are likely to have different assurance requirements to match their individual needs. This is especially true where stakeholders from a number of organisations are coming together to participate in a project. If each stakeholder's assurance requirements are actioned independently, it is likely to engage the project in duplicate effort with no additional benefit. The first dimension for integrated assurance is bringing together the disparate requirements of individual stakeholders and establishing a single set of assurance activities that satisfies the needs of all stakeholders as efficiently as possible.

2. *Governance hierarchy*. A second dimension of integrated assurance derives from applying assurance at the appropriate level in the hierarchy of project, programme or portfolio. Typically, an organisation will run a portfolio of pro-grammes and individual projects. Stakeholders in the organisation itself may be different from stakeholders in specific programmes and individual projects, and each group of stakeholders will have its own assurance require-ments. Without integration an individual project may find itself subjected to assurance processes from a project level, a programme level and a portfolio level – with little co-ordination between them.

3. *Lifecycle stages*. A third dimension of integrated assurance is to recognise that assurance activities will be carried out on a number of occasions throughout the lifecycle of the project and to ensure that the activities on any one occasion are wholly pertinent to that particular stage in the project lifecycle. This also allows linkage to programme lifecycle stages where appropriate.

4. *Level of independence*. The definition of assurance also implies the need for some measure of independence from the team directly managing the project, since lack of such independence would potentially reduce the confidence that stakeholders might have in the assurance reports. In practice, a good project team will carry out certain activities for the purposes of providing assurance to themselves that requirements will be met, as will the project's suppliers. Examples of this would be design verification studies or those activities forming the project's quality management programme. A fourth dimension of integrated assurance would be to recognise those internal and supplier assurance activities, audit them for effectiveness where deemed appropriate, and then overlay a minimum of additional independent assurance needed to provide the appropriate stakeholder confidence that the project will meet all its objectives.

It is worth noting that all assurance activities, whether integrated or not, should be designed with due consideration of project risks, so that assurance resources are applied where the risks are highest.

It should also be noted that assurance is not simply the investigation and reporting of findings. To be effective, assurance needs to include both the identification of actions to address the findings and the subsequent follow-up or consequential assurance to ensure such actions have been effective.

1.2 Overview of the guide

This guide has been developed by APM using the knowledge and experience of project management and assurance providers from across UK industry, the public and third sector, and academia. It has been designed to support those who sponsor or manage projects by describing principles and practices for providing efficient and effective assurance of projects and programmes. It recognises that while projects and programmes will often have multiple stakeholders, each having individual assurance needs that may not be aligned, a planned, integrated programme of assurance should reduce the overall assurance burden.

The guide is consistent with and based on descriptions of assurance as given in the *APM Body of Knowledge* (6th edition). It is also aligned with and builds upon the principles and guidance contained in the APM publication: *Directing Change: A Guide to Governance of Project Management.*

The requirements across UK industry, and the public and third sector have been considered while preparing this guide. It is intended that the guide should be applicable to all such entities. Hence, we refer to 'the organisation' rather than 'the company'.

1.3 Objective of the guide

The objective of this guide is to enable organisations to improve the efficiency and effectiveness of assurance activities such that stakeholders may have more confidence in the successful outcomes of their projects while the cost and negative impacts of assurance will be reduced and the positive impacts will be maximised.

1.4 Target audience for the guide

The target audience for this guide includes those responsible for projects, programmes and portfolios, and project sponsors in particular; those responsible for designing and carrying out assurance activities; and the stakeholders that have an interest in the successful delivery of the projects, programmes or portfolios.

1.5 Scope of the guide

This guide addresses integrated assurance as applicable at the project, programme and portfolio level throughout all stages and important decision points. It is applicable to all types of project, programme and portfolio across all sectors. It describes principles and key concepts but does not attempt to define detailed assurance processes.

1.6 Structure of the guide

Initially, the guide describes some principles that need to be followed to ensure that assurance can be carried out in an integrated manner.

Next, it describes an approach that can be taken to designing and implementing integrated assurance. It is not prescriptive, as every organisation will have its own unique set of assurance challenges to meet. Instead, it talks generally about assurance, guiding the reader in recognising different types and levels of assurance, different types of stakeholder (including both customers and providers of assurance), and obstacles to be overcome.

A roles and responsibilities section enables understanding of how the various people involved in and around a project contribute to its assurance regime.

Finally, two appendices are provided to further assist the reader. Appendix 1 provides some templates that the reader may wish to use. In Appendix 2, there is a glossary of assurance-related terms.

2

Principles

The purpose of defining the principles for integrated assurance is to show how they build on the established principles for assurance generally.

The principles are the fundamental building blocks on which best practice assurance and integrated assurance are established. When applied, the principles form the baseline for ensuring consistency and quality of the process.

Table 2.1 *Principles of integrated assurance*

Principles	Assurance	Integrated assurance
	The process of providing confidence to stakeholders that projects, programmes and portfolios will achieve their scope, time, cost and quality objectives, and realise their benefits (*APM BoK 6th edition*)	The coordination of assurance activities where there are a number of assurance providers (*APM BoK 6th edition*)
Independence	Assurance provides an objective view and conclusion that cannot be influenced, through: • endorsement and support for independence from the most senior level of management in the organisation; • assessors that have no direct project management role, are not stakeholders, and have no ability to control project outcomes or service operations; • data and systems that are unable to be manipulated in support of assurance assessments.	
Accountability	To give assurance due authority there should be: • ownership by the sponsor; • strategic sponsorship and commitment; • a nominated individual with responsibility for assurance within the project; • an appropriate governance and reporting system in place; • trust, transparency and visibility of evidence-based findings.	

Principles	Assurance	Integrated assurance
Planning and coordination	Assurance activities are: • part of an organisation's management system; • planned and agreed with appropriate priorities from the outset of a project; • appropriately funded and resourced; • updated and augmented with consequential assurance.	Through an integrated assurance strategy and plan, assurance: • is developed collaboratively between project and assurance providers to meet stakeholder requirements; • is visible, resources are known and can be costed; • enables the right assurance method to be applied at the right time; • is reviewed and updated to reflect changing environment, risks and earlier assurance findings; • is extendable to, and coordinated with, other assurances within supplier organisations; • facilitates the sharing of appropriate material across the assurance community.
Proportionate	Assurance activities are proportionate to: • risk potential; • the assurance needs of stakeholders.	Integrated assurance: • builds on and does not repeat the work of other assurers; • is tailored to maximise effective use of resources;
Risk-based	Assurance activity is: • based on an independent risk (potential) assessment; • focused on areas of greatest risks to legal, regulatory, investment and performance requirements; • cognisant of specific areas of financial, delivery, technical, social, political, programme, operational and reputational risks.	Integrated assurance coverage is: • agreed between the project, assurance providers and stakeholders; • provided throughout the project lifecycle from concept through to the realisation of benefits.

(Continued)

Table 2.1 *Continued*

Principles	Assurance	Integrated assurance
Impact, follow up and escalation	Assurance should have: • action plans developed to address identified weaknesses; • governance, reporting and escalation routes established.	Integrated assurance should: • share findings between providers and projects; • provide a single view of a project's well-being from assurance providers through aggregated findings; • enable the consolidation of lessons learned; • measure the effectiveness of the integrated assurance provisions.

3

Approach to integrated assurance of projects

3.1 Why do we need assurance?

Assurance is a key element of the governance of a project and it seeks evidence of effective controls and opportunities to increase the likelihood of success in the following areas:

1. *Client and scope*. Focusing on clear and controlled baseline requirements, objectives, success criteria, business case, terms of reference, contracts and benefits realisation.
2. *Risks and opportunities*. Focusing on management of risk and opportunity through the lifecycle of the project.
3. *Planning and scheduling*. Focusing on appropriately detailed execution strategies, plans and schedules.
4. *Organisational capability and culture*. Focusing on people, behaviours, teams, processes, systems and the working environment.
5. *Supply chain*. Focusing on procurement processes, engagement with and capability of both the internal and external supply chain.
6. *Solution*. Focusing on the deliverables and outcomes that meet the client requirements, including product and/or service quality and the impact of the finished product or service on the social, physical and economic environment.
7. *Finance*. Focusing on financial management and administration.
8. *Social responsibility and sustainability*. Focusing on managing the impact of project delivery on the ecological, social, physical and economic environment, including health and safety.
9. *Performance*. Focusing on measuring all facets of performance against the baseline requirements, variance analysis and management action.
10. *Governance*. Focusing on the alignment of the interests and strategic direction of sponsors and stakeholders.

3.2 Who needs assurance?

Assurance is needed by anyone who delegates work to another person/team – whether it is assigned to their own team or to a third party, possibly through a contract. Assurance is also needed by any third parties/stakeholders who will benefit by the work being completed as intended. An example of this might be where the general public will benefit from the launch of a new product but their interests are protected by an industry body or regulator during its development.

These assurance customers can receive assurance that the delegated work is being performed to their requirements by taking an active role in the project and conducting their own reviews. More commonly, this assurance activity is also delegated to assurance providers who are independent of the parties carrying out the delegated work but who report to the assurance customers.

Within an organisation, the board is responsible for assuring that the business is effectively run (in Government this is the accounting officer), that every project is properly governed (see *APM guide: Directing Change – A Guide to Governance of Project Management*), and that every project will deliver the outcomes required. Often this responsibility is supported by a management committee that focuses on delivering projects and business operations to meet organisational standards, risk committee(s) that provide oversight of a risk management framework, and an audit committee that provides independent review and oversight of a company's financial reporting processes and internal controls.

Normally, a board will assign the governance of a project to a sponsor who is responsible for ensuring that the project leads to the intended outcomes, and this involves ensuring that the appropriate assurance activities are performed for that project. For portfolio or programme, there may be a number of interdependent projects and related activities resulting in a hierarchy of management to be assured about the results of the work in each programme and project.

In addition to this assurance, a board will normally have an internal audit department (or equivalent) who will independently assure that the organisation's activities, including projects, are appropriately governed and assured. Traditionally, an audit/assurance department consists largely of people whose background was accounting. However, with increasing investment in projects and programmes of change (and for other reasons too), a board needs broader skills in their audit/assurance function so that the various complexities of a project can be properly assessed and assured in addition to the financial aspects.

In addition, projects often find themselves with a multitude of stakeholders who may wish to gain oversight on the health of a project. These stakeholders often employ more than one specialist agency to perform assurance on their behalf. Stakeholders and the agencies they employ may include:

Table 3.1 *Stakeholders and agencies employed*

Stakeholders	Examples of assurance providers
Parliament	National Audit Office
Local and Central Government, and other public bodies	Major Projects Authority/Cabinet Office/local partnerships
Funders and investors	Financial advisers
Regulatory agencies	Own and third-party auditors/inspectors
End user	Own and third-party auditors
Client organisation (NB: There may be more than one client within an organisation.)	Clients: • Internal audit • Financial compliance • Governance • Gated reviews • Value for money • Third-party auditors • Project management office • Project managers
Client organisation's operational and support functions	Functional review/audit teams: • Health & Safety • Environment • Technical
Client organisation's project management team	Project management teams: • Management systems/quality assurance team • Functional review/audit teams • Third-party auditors
Suppliers (NB: The supplier's senior executive, who is responsible for the successful delivery of the project, acts as the 'sponsor' for delivery of the scope in accordance with the supplier's contract.)	Supplier's corporate • Internal audit • Financial compliance • Governance • Gated reviews • Value for money • Management systems/quality assurance team • Third-party auditors • Functional review/audit teams • Project management office • Project managers

(Continued)

Table 3.1 *Continued*

Stakeholders	Examples of assurance providers
	Supplier's contract
	• Management systems/quality assurance team
Other stakeholders – those affected during delivery or benefiting on completion	Own and third-party auditors

3.3 How is assurance organised and performed?

Traditionally, the client's project management team, stakeholders and the sponsor each arrange their own assurance activities. As a result, projects may become burdened with assurance interventions that may not necessarily provide the assurance required. If a serious problem arises, all the stakeholders and their respective assurance providers may want to get involved. This can lead to significant overheads for the project team, with inconsistent analyses of the problem.

It is the role of the sponsor to set expectations regarding the sharing of assurance information, liaise with all of the stakeholders, and present to the stakeholders and to the project team on their behalf, a single voice in terms of assurance requirements, priorities and, when necessary, change. It is the sponsor who should take the initiative to ensure that a plan is created and implemented on behalf of all stakeholders that:

- addresses the ten areas listed under the section 'Why do we need assurance?' above;
- is aligned with the project schedule so that assurance interventions take place at an appropriate point in time;
- takes account of reporting cycles and gateway or other reviews that may be scheduled as part of the project's governance arrangements so that the assurance information that these provide is taken into account.

The challenge facing all projects is to understand and organise assurance activities. This begins with a shared understanding of assurance needs and knowledge of who provides assurance. Assurance services can then be organised in a cost-effective way with clarity on how and when they will be provided.

Above all, the process should ensure there is sufficient assurance on the things that matter. Key factors to be considered will include:

- the requirements of the primary or commissioning customer;
- agreed risk levels (individual projects and the programme as a whole);
- *ad hoc* concerns or critical delivery confidence issues;
- specific programme/project characteristics;
- availability of assurance specialist skills and capacity;
- allowance within project plans for the assurance activities.

The way in which assurance can be performed needs to be carefully planned and managed because:

- In order to keep the overall costs down, the costs of assurance must be appropriate compared to the costs of the project and the risks involved.
- It is impossible to accurately assess the likelihood or exact impact of a risk, so whether objectives will be met is a subjective analysis.

Assurance must be focused on those areas where there is the highest risk of project failure, thus increasing the effectiveness of the assurance process. Assurance is best performed by experienced professionals who have the knowledge and skills to ensure that the assurance work is scoped effectively.

It is also preferable that any assurance activities are performed by people who are independent and objective (i.e. they have no involvement in the delivery of the work) so that the assurance findings are evidence based and not relying on the same, possibly mistaken, assumptions of others.

Organising the different sources of assurance within a single model can provide the basis for a better understanding and organisation of assurance, while creating a platform for coordination. The 'three lines of defence' model, which is illustrated and explained overleaf, is recommended as a means to develop a framework of defence against the constant threat of evolving risks.

In the model shown, the lines of defence are:

First line of defence: Controls within systems and processes operated by managers and staff with direct responsibility for controlling risks.

These are the day-to-day systems and processes that exist to keep projects under control, and are usually described within the project's management system.

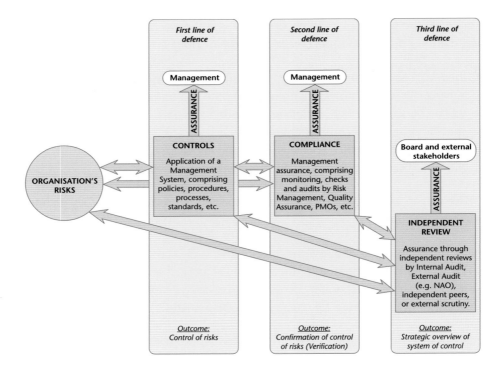

Figure 3.1 *The 'three lines of defence' model for assurance*

Second line of defence: Independent checks for compliance and effectiveness with the first line systems and processes

This involves reviews conducted by people independent of the project to ensure that controls are not being bypassed or incorrectly operated. These reviews are typically carried out by the project's/organisation's compliance and risk management functions.

Third line of defence: Independent assurance in respect of the effectiveness of governance, risk management and controls.

This involves independent assurance to the board, usually provided by the board's internal audit/assurance and external audit/assurance agencies.

The extent of assurance performed at this level will depend on the existence and effectiveness of the first and second lines. The third line of defence should also seek to identify strengths and weaknesses in both the first and second lines of defence and place reliance on their work where effectively carried out, rather than seek to duplicate it.

The precise application of this model to any project will vary depending on the nature of the assurance functions that exist. It should be used only as a basis for understanding the relative roles of each function, not for rigidly defining an assurance regime. Furthermore, the application may need to change from time to time to reflect changes in risks, assurance needs and organisation.

In order to formulate and coordinate assurance needs, project teams must have a comprehensive understanding of their:

- principal objectives and benefits required;
- acceptance criteria and acceptable tolerances;
- principal risks;
- key processes and controls (usually documented in a management system).

To assist in the understanding of how each assurance provider will provide assurance in respect of each risk, it may help to prepare a 'risk and assurance matrix', a template for which is provided in Table A1 (Section A1.1).

3.4 Why integrated assurance?

Assurance is especially important at key milestones or decision points (e.g. investment decision points) during a project. However, assurance can be performed at any time in order to assess whether the intended processes are being followed and contemporary records are created that show that activities that ought to have been done have been done and done correctly, and whether the project is appropriately managing its risks and issues in seeking to deliver its benefits within time, cost and quality parameters.

A key element of assurance is the preparation of an assurance plan that defines which assurance activities are to be performed at which times during a project.

Most projects will be impacted by external factors during their lifetime and so the project's assurance plan needs to remain 'dynamic' and be continuously reviewed throughout the life of the project.

3.5 How to implement integrated assurance on a project

The amount and type of assurance of a project should be a judgement by the sponsor about what investment they should make in assurance activities in order to be confident of success, given the risks of the project and the capabilities of the team. This guide recommends the following approach to integrated assurance be adopted by the sponsor of a project:

1. The stakeholders, under the leadership of the sponsor, and taking account of the organisation's integrated assurance strategy (see Appendix 1, Section A1.2), define
   a. the project objectives and success criteria, (i.e. the benefits that will accrue once the project deliverable is in place);
   b. the requirements (e.g. health, safety, environmental impact, schedule, budget, functional and operational characteristics, technical standards and aesthetics) that the project must fulfil to enable achievement of the objectives;
   c. identify the benefits and the risks to delivering them and consider the different types of assurance that are available and required for this project and prepare a risk and assurance matrix, aligned to the organisation's strategy.
2. The supplier(s) define their risk and other management processes and reporting. Strong processes with adequate reporting should give the stakeholders greater confidence, requiring fewer assurance interventions from second and third lines of defence.
3. Based on the above, the stakeholders, under the leadership of the sponsor, should identify a lead assurance provider who facilitates bringing the various assurance providers for the stakeholders together to:
   a. Use an approach such as the three lines of defence model to produce an integrated assurance plan (see Appendix 1, Section A1.3), balancing the needs of the project, the stakeholders and the risks involved. The plan should show all the assurance activities and which assurance agency will perform them and when.
   b. Agree that the project's risk and other management processes are adequate/appropriate.
   c. Agree the project reporting requirements and the level of assurance required to give confidence in the project reports.

    d. Agree the escalation route for the resolution of any assurance issues identified.

    e. Seek approval, at an appropriate level, that the plan and an integrated assurance approach will be adopted.

    f. Decide which assurance provider is right for which piece of assurance and decide on joint teams where appropriate

4. During the project, based on the results of the assurance and any changes to the project or its risks, the assurance plan needs to be updated.

3.6 Other considerations for a programme or portfolio

A programme often is of much greater complexity than a project, so greater effort needs to be applied to assurance activities. Each project within the programme will normally have its own assurance activities as described above, plus the programme will have some staff assigned to assure that the projects are working in tandem and that the overall benefits will be achieved as expected.

Each project in a portfolio should be assured as described above. Some portfolios have an independent set of projects, but usually there is some dependency between projects. Hence, like a programme, the portfolio management should assign some staff to assure that the relevant projects are working in a co-ordinated fashion and that the overall benefits will be achieved as expected. The assurance approach to be applied to all projects and programmes within a portfolio should be recorded within the organisation's integrated assurance strategy (see Appendix 1, Section A1.2). Many portfolios and programmes will also have non-project elements – assurance over which needs to be taken account.

Barriers to integrated assurance

It is essential that the sponsor has a clear understanding of what assurance is required and who is providing it. Recognising this responsibility and the compelling nature of the benefits of integrated assurance, why does it seem so hard to deliver? The main obstacles to the coordination of assurance are:

- a lack of board and senior management understanding of and commitment to integrated assurance, mitigated by engaging with members of the senior management and explaining the benefits of integrated assurance;

- no one has ownership, mitigated by the role and responsibilities for the sponsor being clearly defined, including their responsibility for assurance;
- the different terminology and methods of assurance providers, mitigated by the lead assurance coordinator role ensuring these are agreed in the integrated assurance plan;
- the risk management framework is not sufficiently developed, mitigated by engaging with senior management to explain the benefits of having a risk management framework and clear risk sponsorship;
- the self interest of the different assurance providers, mitigated by the integrated assurance plan clearly defining the roles and responsibilities of each assurance provider, how these inter-relate and how they should work together;
- the competency and skills of assurance providers, mitigated by the integrated assurance plan clearly defining the skills and experience necessary for the assurance providers;
- a lack of trust between assurance providers, mitigated by the development of an agreed integrated assurance plan detailing the roles and responsibilities of each assurance provider including where information should be shared;
- assurance is based on opinions and these will vary, mitigated by development of an agreed integrated assurance plan detailing standards to be used by each assurance provider.

Good practices

Here are a few examples of good practice in applying integrated assurance.

- Every project sponsor should have a clear view (preferably as a risk and assurance matrix) of the project assurance that is in place, or proposed, so they can judge, in changing circumstances, whether the assurance regime meets their needs and that of all the external stakeholders.
- The 'right' level of assurance should be developed 'top-down' and be 'risk-based'. No two projects are likely to require exactly the same structure. Project teams, in consultation with assurance providers, should develop the assurance plan, on behalf of their sponsors, in line with the organisation's assurance strategy.
- An integrated assurance plan should seek to assure the achievement of business or policy outcomes and benefits as well as the delivery of outputs. Thus, it must cover business change activities as well as project deliverables.
- Projects should, as far as possible, recognise the cost of assurance, and should make provision for and track the time and cost involved.

- An integrated assurance plan and all assurance results should be shared across all stakeholders, providing visibility, transparency and developing trust across both the project team and the assurance providers within the constraints of the organisation and/or contractual obligations.
- The number of assurance interventions will be reduced if the project follows good practices and provides accurate management information to all parties. Hence, the first assurance activity should be to review and advise on the adequacy of the project's practices and management information.

4

Roles and responsibilities in the context of integrated assurance

Table 4.1 details typical roles and responsibilities in the context of integrated assurance. However, each member brings with them their individual responsibilities from their respective functional disciplines to support the aims of the integrated assurance team.

Table 4.1 *Roles and responsibilities*

Role	Responsibilities pertaining to integrated assurance
Executive/ board	• Initiate, approve and oversee the organisation's assurance strategy • Provide senior management commitment to undertaking assurance activities and to acting on recommendations
Sponsor/senior responsible owner (SRO)	• Responsible for providing funders and other stakeholders with the confidence that the project can deliver to time, budget and quality and also to alert them if there are any problems to delivery • Ensure there is commitment to the integrated assurance plan, and that it is produced to address primary risks and delivers the requirements of the integrated assurance strategy once approved • Analyse assurance business reporting data and provide management overview, direction and intervention as required
Portfolio manager	• Ensure that the executive/board and stakeholders receive the right data upon which to base critical business decisions • Co-ordinate the successful delivery of the integrated assurance plan across the portfolio • Organise and manage assurance reviews in line with the integrated assurance plan • Monitor assurance review outputs and ensure appropriate management intervention occurs at the programme and project level

Role	Responsibilities pertaining to integrated assurance
Support office or equivalent	• Deliver a project governance and management infrastructure that demonstrably meets the assurance requirements and customer specific delivery requirements • Ensure adherence to assurance plans in response to assurance manager requirements • Provide secretariat support to assurance review meetings and monitor assurance deliverables
Project/ programme manager	• Deliver project assurance objectives pertinent to the project manager's objectives • Apply knowledge and skill, along with specific tools and techniques, to support delivery of assurance objectives
Functional/ team lead	Provide subject matter expertise to deliver assurance activities as directed by the project manager
Project team member	Supporting the portfolio, programme and/or project manager
Assurance manager/ assurance provider	• Advise on assurance methodologies and best practice as the assurance subject matter expert across the portfolio and advise the executive/board • Independently evaluate, through audit and provision of objective evidence, overall project assurance performance in support of assurance reviews
Stakeholders	Have a vested interest in the assurance of delivery of benefits and outcomes of the portfolio and programmes

5

Further reading

1. The Audit Commission and their document entitled *Taking It on Trust*, published in April 2009. The website includes a governance checklist for self-assessment that can be adapted for most organisations, a presentation and a number of case studies.
2. National Audit Office report, June 2010, *Assurance for High Risk Projects*.
3. HM Treasury and Cabinet Office, April 2011, *Major Project Approval and Assurance Guidance*.
4. National Audit Office report, May 2012, *Assurance for Major Projects*.
5. Lord Browne report, March 2013, *Getting a Grip: How to Improve Major Project Execution and Control in Government*.
6. The Department of Health document, *Building the Assurance Framework*, published in March 2003. This site also includes *The Assurance Framework and the Statement on Internal Control*.
7. The Institute of Chartered Accountants England & Wales (ICAEW) Technical Release AAF 01/06. *Assurance Reports on Internal Controls of Service Organisations*, made available to third parties.
8. The King Code of Governance for South Africa, September 2009, available from the European Corporate Governance Institute. A summary is available from the global *IIA Internal Auditor Magazine*.
9. The Office of Government Commerce has produced *Lessons Learned – Effective Project Assurance*. This explains the role and benefits of assurance and gives examples of good practice.
10. The Association for Project Management's publication, *Directing Change: A Guide to Governance of Project Management*.
11. The Association for Project Management's publication, *Sponsoring Change – A Guide to the Governance Aspects of Project Sponsorship*.
12. British Standard, *Guidelines for Managing Audit Systems* (BS EN ISO 19011:2011).

APPENDIX 1
Tools and templates

This appendix contains three tools that can be used to facilitate the development and implementation of integrated assurance:

- Risk and assurance matrix
- Integrated assurance strategy
- Integrated assurance plan

A1.1 Risk and assurance matrix

The risk and assurance matrix (Table A1) is a simple tool that shows how, at a high level, assurance will be provided for each of the associated risks.

Along one side of the matrix, the risks over which assurance is required are listed. Along the other, the various assurance providers/sources (usually arranged around the three-lines-of-defence model) are shown. Where it is planned that a particular provider/source will provide assurance over a particular risk, an indication of this is shown in the matrix.

Not only is the tool useful in presenting a simple high-level assurance 'picture', it also provides an effective and straightforward planning tool in helping to ensure that all of the risks requiring assurance are adequately covered, and that there is no unnecessary duplication.

Table A1 *Risk and assurance matrix for Project X*

Risk description	First line			Second line				Third line		
	Management actions and reporting	Programme boards and reviews (inc 'the plan')	The management system	Risk management	Quality assurance	HSE assurance	Project assurance	Internal audit	External scrutiny	External audits
Risk 1	✓	✓	✓	✓			✓	✓		✓
Risk 2	✓	✓		v				✓		
Risk 3	✓	✓	✓	✓				✓		
Risk 4	✓	✓		✓				✓		
Risk 5	✓			✓				✓		
Risk 6	✓	✓		✓				✓		
Risk 7	✓	✓	✓	✓			✓	✓		
Risk 8	✓	✓		✓			✓	✓		
Risk 9	✓	✓		✓			✓	✓		
Risk 10	✓	✓		✓				✓		✓
Risk 11	✓	✓		✓				✓		
Risk 12	✓			✓				✓		

A1.2 Integrated assurance strategy

The following is a suggested contents list and structure for an integrated assurance strategy (IAS).

Introduction

- What an IAS is
- Its objectives

Purpose and scope

- How the IAS will be used within the organisation
- Scope of the IAS, including any exclusions or exceptions
- Reference to the organisation's requirements for integrated assurance plans (IAPs)

Application of assurance

- A commitment to end-to-end, risk-based, integrated assurance across the organisation
- A commitment to use established best practice, e.g. planned and consequential assurance and escalation processes where appropriate
- A short summary outlining and endorsing the tools and techniques to be used, i.e. IAPs, corporate functional assurance, audit, etc.

Approvals

- Why and how assurance processes must be linked to the approvals processes within the organisation

Responsibilities and accountabilities

- A description of the organisation's strategic assurance responsibilities and accountability model – including validation processes for IAPs
- Principles for how assurance must be applied, e.g. timely, best practice, etc.
- Statement of relevant sponsor responsibilities, including dissemination of assurance review reports so that all interested parties are kept informed, and implementation of the actions and recommendations in such reports.

Reporting and communications

- A description of the reporting processes, tools and schedules to be used – both internal and external
- The corporate approach to, and means of, communicating outcomes (both positive and negative) from assurance activity, both internally and externally
- Transparency requirements and commitments in relation to assurance outcomes and reports.

Resourcing

- Commitment to develop a pool of resources for deployment on assurance reviews
- Show the relationship between assurance review participation and the individual's learning and development and with the corporate PPM capability enhancement
- Corporate recognition of assurance reviewer expertise and contribution.

A1.3 Integrated assurance plan

The following is a suggested contents list and structure for an integrated assurance plan (IAP).

Introduction

- Reference to the corporate IAS
- What an IAP is
- Its objectives

Purpose and scope

- How the IAP will be used by the project team
- Scope of the IAP, including any exclusions and exceptions
- Reference to the organisation's requirements for IAPs

Assessment of risks and determination of assurance requirements

- Tools and techniques used to determine risk and focus for assurance activities
- Description of how the IAP has been developed

Roles and responsibilities

- Identify who within the organisation has what responsibilities in relation to assurance
- List of additional key stakeholders and interested parties

Planned assurance coverage and scheduling

- Description of the assurance products to be used
- When and why they are to be used

Cost and resources

- An estimate of chargeable costs required for all assurance activities for the period of the plan
- An indication of project resources requirements for assurance activities

Reporting and communications

- A description of the reporting processes, tools and schedules to be used – both internal and external
- The project approach to, and means of, communicating outcomes (whether positive or negative) from assurance activity, both internally and externally
- Transparency requirements and commitments in relation to assurance outcomes and reports

Managing outcomes, consequential assurance and escalation

- Sponsor responsibility for implementing the actions and recommendations in the assurance review reports
- Overall approach to acting on assurance findings
- Processes and tools to be used in different circumstances

Schedule

- The planned assurance activities for a minimum of (for example) two years ahead
- Assurance links to approval paths and key milestones

APPENDIX 2
Glossary

Risk and assurance matrix

The risk and assurance matrix is a tool that shows how, at a high level, assurance will be provided for each of the associated risks within a project.

Integrated assurance plan (IAP)

A document that determines what is to be assured, when it will be assured, how it will be assured and who will carry out the assurance. This document delivers the requirements of the integrated assurance strategy.

Integrated assurance strategy (IAS)

A document that sets the strategic requirements for assurance provision to ensure agreed and consistent standards across an organisation's portfolio of projects.

Consequential assurance

An assurance activity that results from earlier assurance where a project is considered to be in difficulty.

Planned assurance

Assurance activities that are known in advance, usually linked to a key decision point, approval or milestone.